Still Life in Milford

Poetry

Skating with Heather Grace (1987)
Grimalkin & Other Poems (1994)

Essays

The Undertaking—Life Studies from the Dismal Trade (1997)

Still Life in Milford

POEMS BY

THOMAS LYNCH

W. W. Norton & Company   *New York • London*

Copyright © 1998 by Thomas Lynch

All rights reserved
Printed in the United States of America
First Edition

For information about permission to reproduce selections from this book,
write to Permissions, W. W. Norton & Company, Inc., 500 Fifth Avenue,
New York, NY 10110

The text of this book is composed in Fairfield Light
Desktop composition by Julia Druskin
Manufacturing by The Courier Companies, Inc.
Book design by Chris Welch

Library of Congress Cataloging-in-Publication Data

Lynch, Thomas, 1948–
    Still life in Milford : poems / by Thomas Lynch.
        p. cm.
    ISBN 0-393-04659-1
    1. Milford (Mich.)—Poetry. 2. Death—Poetry. I. Title.
PS3562.Y437S75   1998
811'.54—dc21   98-5934
                                                    CIP

W. W. Norton & Company, Inc., 500 Fifth Avenue, New York, N.Y. 10110
http://www.wwnorton.com

W. W. Norton & Company Ltd., 10 Coptic Street, London, WC1A 1PU

1 2 3 4 5 6 7 8 9 0

*This book is for Mary Tata
and for Tom, Heather, Michael & Sean Lynch*

Contents

Acknowledgments

Some poems here originally appeared in the following publications, to whose editors the author expresses his thanks:

Cuirt Literary Journal (Galway), *Cyphers* (Dublin), *The Gettysburg Review, The Honest Ulsterman* (Belfast), *The Irish Times, London Magazine, The New Yorker, The Paris Review, The Poetry Review* (London), *Poetry Ireland Review, Poetry Wales, The Quarterly, River Styx, The Southern Review, Virginia Quarterly Review, Visions International,* and *Witness.*

"Grimalkin," "Kisses," "Liberty," "An Evening Walk to the Sea by Friesians," "Heavenward," "The Nines," and "At the Opening of Oak Grove Cemetery Bridge" were broadcast on BBC Radio 4 on "Stanza on Stage," for which the author thanks Kate McAll, producer.

"The Old Operating Theatre, London, All Souls Night" appears in Waterstone's Books Poetry Catalogue, fall, 1996 London.

"Still Life in Milford—Oil on Canvas by Lester Johnson" appears in *A Visit to the Gallery,* University of Michigan Press, 1996. Richard Tillinghast, editor.

Some of the poems collected here appeared in *Grimalkin & Other Poems* (Jonathan Cape, London, 1994), to whose editor, Robin Robertson, the author wishes to make known his permanent indebtedness.

The author is likewise beholding to Jill Bialosky, Richard McDonough, Matthew Sweeney, Michael Heffernan, Audrey Kowalski, Melissa Weisberg, Colleen Reader, and Mary Tata for their early knowledge of and interest in these poems.

"At the Opening of Oak Grove Cemetery Bridge" is dedicated to Mary Jackson, "That Scream if You Ever Hear It" to Gordon Lish, "The Lives of Women" to June Levine, "Bishop's Island" to P. J. & Breda Roche, "St. James Park Epistle" to Nell Cooke-Hurle, "Still Life in Milford" to Keith Taylor, "Loneliest of Trees, The Winter Oak" to Caitlin Lynch.

Still Life in Milford

I

Subject matter per se *is secondary; primary is the
projection of a personal but broadly significant vision,
based at once on a physical intimacy with and a
metaphysical distance from the real world.*
    —Exhibition Guide, "Objects of Desire: The Modern Still Life"
                                Hayward Gallery, London, 1997

*It is difficult to make moral or intellectual claims for
any arrangement of fruit or vegetables on a table . . .*
                                        —Richard R. Brettell
                        "Impressionist Still Life" in *French Impressionists,*
                                The Art Institute of Chicago, 1987

Art History, Chicago

It's not so much a *Sunday Afternoon*
on the Island of La Grande Jatte as the point
of order according to Seurat—
that bits of light and color, oil paints
aligned in dots become the moment caught,
verbs slowed to a standstill, the life examined.
We step back wide-eyed for a better look:
an assemblage of Parisian suburbanites
in Sunday dress, top hats and parasols,
are there among the trees beside the river
There are girls and women, men and dogs
in random attitudes of ease and leisure.
A stretch of beach, boats in the blue water,
a woman with a monkey on a leash,
a stiff man beside her, a mother and daughter,
that little faceless girl who seems to look at us.
And everyone is slightly overdressed except
for a boatman stretched out in the shade.
He smokes his pipe and waits for passengers.

But I have never been to Paris.
I've never holidayed beside the Seine
nor strolled with a French girl in the gray morning
as in this *Paris Street, A Rainy Day*—
Gustave Caillebotte's earlier masterpiece
three galleries down in this collection.

So I do not know these cobblestones, this street,
this corner this couple seems intent on turning.
But I've walked with a woman arm in arm
holding an umbrella in a distant city,
and felt the moment quicken, yearning for
rainfall or a breeze off the river or
the glistening flesh of her body in water
the way this woman's is about to be
that Degas has painted in *The Morning Bath*.
She rises from her bed, removes her camisole
and steps into the tub a hundred years ago.

History's a list of lovers and cities,
a mention of the weather, names and dates
of meetings in libraries and museums
of walks by the sea, or through a city,
late luncheons, long conversations, memories
of what happened or what didn't happen.
But art is the brush of a body on your body,
the permanent impression that the flesh
retains of courtesies turned intimate;
the image and likeness, the record kept
of figures emergent in oil or water
by the river, in the rain or in the bath
when, luminous with love and its approval,
that face, which you hardly ever see,
turns its welcome towards you yet again.

Attende Domine

To lie in the tub on New Year's morning
awash in bath oil and resolution,
observing the Feast of the Circumcision,
is to seek the water's absolution
according to the law that juxtaposes
Cleanliness and Godliness. I suppose
it is time to examine my conscience,
to make a clean breast of it and amends
to such as those I might have offended.
Attende Domine et miserere! Lord
I've sinned with my eye and did not pluck it out,
and with my hand and yet my hand remains
blessing myself against Your righteousness.
I've sinned with my mouth and loved the sound it made.

Vigil

Rose, you are the winter oak
whose spent leaves redden and remain
limp emblems of the heart's accustomed hold
on this—the known life of seasons,
daylights, nightfalls, weathers—
the ordinary calendars, mean time.
Ordinarily we live our lives out
hopeful and afloat among the rounded metaphors:
seedtime and harvest, dark and dawn;
solstice and equinox, calm, storm.
Ignoring the linear paradigms we move
buoyantly between our pasts and futures
gamely trading prospects for remembrances,
deaf to the regular changing of tenses—
those doorways slamming down the narrowing hall.
Behind the doors, we hear the voices still:
Goodnight. Godspeed. God Bless. Get Well. Goodbye.
The deaths we seldom grieve but set our watches by.

Pange Lingua

This is the voice I talk to myself in.
The one that says, before I fall asleep,
the children will all grow up and outlive me;
my mother's tumor will be benign;
the women who loved me will always love me.
This is the same voice I heard as a child
the time I first ate meat on a Friday,
at Bobby Bacon's house. It said, "Baloney."
Or when I lingered over magazines
Jim Shryock and I found stashed in his basement—
conscience and complicity: the voice that sings
Pange Lingua in the shower nowadays,
sings the glorious body's mystery,
of blood and bliss and love and misery.

Late April

Six months to the morning since the day you died.
Another heartsore Friday full of sun,
temps in the sixties, a stirring in the trees.
We have put a winter in between our griefs—
between the gaping hole and greening sod,
between the wet funeral and dry one.

There was a comfort in the numbers then.
We counted priests and limousines, flowers,
favors, the sympathies and casseroles
of those who came and followed to the end
in keeping with the common sense that holds
a strength in numbers: the more the merrier.

Late April now and now the number One
assumes its upright stance—the walking wound
that pauses among monuments to count
another season's emblements of loss:
one grave, one stone, one name on it, one rose,
one fist to shake in the face of God then go.

Inviolata

I had a nunnish upbringing. I served
six-twenty Mass on weekdays for a priest
who taught me the *Confetior* and to keep
a running tally of the things I'd done
against the little voice in me the nuns
were always saying I should listen to.
And listen is what I did and spoke the truth
of it to Father Kenny in confession,
and walked out with a clean slate, listening,
listening. At thirteen what it said was "Tits"
Tits everywhere. Even Sister Jean Therese—
Inviolata, integra, et casta—
for all her blue habits and scapular,
standing at the blackboard, sideways, couldn't hide them.

Green Bananas

My father quit buying
green bananas
for what he said were the
obvious reasons.
And made no plans, the seasons
giving way to days or parts of days
spent waiting for the deadly embolus
the doctors always talked about
to lodge
itself sideways
in some important spot
between his last breath and the one
that would not be coming after that.
Then he said "Let's
go out for Chinese."
He had won-ton soup, eggrolls,
sweet and sour,
grinned when he opened the fortune
cookie, winked at the waitress,
left her a huge tip.
Was dead inside a month.

Panis Angelicus

Sister Jean Therese sold pagan babies
at five dollars a copy. I bought four.
And named them after saints and archangels
and waited for their letters. I suppose
if I haven't heard by now I never will.
Still, who's to know? Stranger things have happened.
Maybe they'll be on the next boat over.
The idea was to save their bodies
and then to claim their souls for Jesus Christ.
The old *Panis Angelicus*, bowl of rice
routine. The loaves and fishes sleight of hand
that feeds the hungry, clothes the bare naked,
relieves them of their dear idolatries—
their fierce gods everywhere, gods in everything.

No Prisoners

Odds are the poor man was trying to please her
because her pleasure would have pleasured him,
adding as it would have to his image of
himself as a latter-day Man of Steel,
able as always to leap tall buildings
and off of whose chest the bullets would bounce,
his five bypasses notwithstanding,
nor withstanding how his heart had grown
flimsy with hard loving and bereavement.
Or maybe it was the Marine Lance Corporal
in the snapshot of himself in the South Pacific
he kept in the corner of the bathroom mirror:
barechested in khakis and boondockers
with Billy Swinford Smith from Paris, Kentucky,
posing as always for the girls back home;
the ready and willing eighteen-year-old
who went from right tackle with St. Francis DeSalles
to light machine gunner with the Corps
and came home skinny and malarial later
to marry the redheaded girl of his dreams
who had written him daily through the war,
beginning her letters with *My Darling Edward*
and closing with *All My Love Always, Rose*.
We found those letters, years later, in a drawer
and tried to imagine them both young again,
dancing to Dorsey and Glenn Miller tunes

under the stars at the Walled Lake Pavilion
before they had any idea of us.
"Six sons," he'd laugh, "enough for pallbearers!
And girls enough to keep us in old age."
So when our mother took to her bed with cancer,
it was, of course, the girls who tended her
while my brothers and I sat with him downstairs,
being brave for each other. When she died
he knelt by her bedside sobbing, "Rosie,
my darling, what will I do without you?"
And grieved his grief like Joe DiMaggio
who never missed a game and took a rose
to place in the vase at her graveside daily
then came home to sit in his chair and weep,
those first nights without her thereby replacing
as the worst in his life a night in '44
on Walt's Ridge in Cape Glouster, New Britain,
when he and elements of the First Marines
survived nine Bonzai charges. The Japanese
foot soldiers kept screaming, kept coming, blind
into the crossfire of light machine guns
that he and Billy and Donald Crescent Coe
kept up all night, aiming just below the voices.
In the morning he crawled out of his hole
to poke his bayonet among the dead
for any signs of life and souvenirs.
Whatever he found, he took no prisoners
and always said he wondered after that
how many men he'd killed, how he'd survived.
He'd try to make some sense of all of it,

but if he did, he never told us what it was.
And now he is dying of heartache and desire.
Six months into his mourning he became
an object of pursuit among the single set
of widows and divorcées hereabouts;
the hero of a joke his cronies tell
that always ends *But what a way to go!*
Last night, mistaking breathlessness for afterglow,
a woman nearly finished him with love
and barely made it to the hospital
where they thumped his chest and ordered oxygen.
The First Marines are off to war again.
He watches CNN in ICU
while Leathernecks dig trenches in the sand.
The president says "No More Vietnams."
The doctors tell him "Easy Does It, Ed—
six weeks, six months, who knows. It's up to you.
Avoid excitement, stimulation, sex
with any but familiar partners."
He tells them "War is Hell. It takes no prisoners.
A man must have something worth dying for."
The Persian skies are bright with bombs and fire.
My father's sleep is watched by monitors
that beep and blink—his sore heart beating, still.
I wonder if he dreams of soldiers killed
in action—Japanese, Iraqis, old Marines
who died for flags and causes, but in the end,
among their souvenirs, we only find
old snapshots of their wives and women friends.

O Gloriosa Virginum

Truth is, I envied those pagan babies
their plentiful deities—lords in stones
and trees, goddesses of hunt and lovemaking,
their dancing liturgies in dryseason.
I envied their bodies, hungry and naked,
their bare-breasted women, unbraided hair
like the women in Jimmy Shryock's magazines
with the look of knowledge on their faces.
What I wanted was to be hungry and naked
with someone, anyone, Sister Jean Therese,
or the dark-haired girl in the front row—O
Gloriosa Virginum! And yet we seemed
sublime amid the stars, somehow at odds
with our own bright bodies and our bodies' gods.

Month's Mind

In the dream you are dead again in Florida.
The long-anticipated phone call comes.
Minced fact—he's gone—and reverent detail:
something acute and myocardial
and after a good day combing the beach
collecting seashells for the grandchildren.
Waking, I trade panic for odd relief:
dead now a month, you cannot die again.

Parce Domine

Maybe I oughtn't to be naming names.
Maybe Sister Jean Therese is still alive,
married to a former priest or nine to five
with one of those human-service agencies.
Maybe Bobby Bacon lives on fruits and cheese
or joined some eastern cult of vegetables.
Maybe Jimmy Shryock works the vice patrol
or has a TV ministry. Who knows?
I know Father Kenny retired to Salthill
and died of eighty years. As for the rest,
maybe I should have used an alias.
Maybe what I should have said was *breasts*
though tits is what they seemed and ever shall seem
world without end. *Parce Domine mei.*

Casablanca

It is always an airport
or a railway station
or one of those airy dockside rooms
folks wait in watching for the boats that move
on schedule between the outer islands.
I'm home from the big war
or a concert tour.
The news is full of my vast heroics.
One of my entourage has gone for the limo.
Another is waiting at the baggage claim.
I'm considering titles for the movie version.
And there you are, there you are, again.
Having finished your work here you have come to book
your passage on the next departure.
You are more beautiful than ever.
All of the men who loved you are dead or vanished.
I am the last man on the face of the century.

Veni Creator Spiritus

And spare me Lord, likewise, my memory of
a woman's body rising from the bath—
the diamond water shining on her back
and how she turned towards me, the way that Eve
most surely turned towards Adam in her flesh
before embarrassment or baptism or death,
before love meant a willingness to die
or gibbet of the cross, before the wine
got consecrated in blood—Good Christ—
before the fall, the flood and days of wrath,
before the latter sacraments of death.
Veni, Creator Spiritus, create
once more the body's easy mystery:
the water, water; the wine, wine; the bread, bread only.

Rhododendrons

It was the dream
I was allowed
to touch you in.
We were strangers.
You kept your eyes closed.
I cannot really say
if there were rhododendrons
or anything like music or
even if I asked you.
Only your blue skin
and the pleasure it gave you—
the way you moved,
the way you caught your breath
whenever my hands moved
so I kept on moving them.

Adoro Te Devote

Father Kenny taught me Latin hymns.
And, lost for words, I'd often chant Gregorian:
Adoro te devote, latens Deitas—
a second tongue, more humbly to adore them in,
those hidden deities: the bodies of women,
the bodies of men, their sufferings and passions,
the sacred mysteries of life and death
by which our sight and touch and taste are all deceived.
By hearing only safely we believe.
And so I listened and am still listening.
I've heard the prayers said over open graves
and heard the pleas of birth and lovemaking.
"O God! O God!" we always seem to say.
And God, God help us, answers "Wait and see."

Kisses

My father turns up in a dream,
sometimes on roller skates, sometimes
in wing-tipped shoes. He's smiling,
impeccably dressed, himself again.
I am delighted to see him.
Maybe I was only dreaming
is what I tell myself inside the dream.
No, he assures me wordlessly.
The facts are still the facts. He's dead.
He and my mother have been to the movies.
She's gone on ahead of him to make the coffee.
He lets me hold him, hug him,
weep some, wake repaired again,
says he'll take my kisses home to her.

In Paradisum

Sometimes I look into the eyes of corpses.
They are like mirrors broken, frozen pools
or empty tabernacles, doors left open,
vacant and agape; like votives cooling,
motionless as stone in their cold focus.
As if they'd seen something. As if it all
came clear to them, at long last, in that last moment
of light perpetual or else the black
abyss of requiems and nothingness.
Only the dead know what the vision is,
beholding which they wholly faint away
amid their plenary indulgences.
In Paradisum, deducant te we pray:
their first sight of what is or what isn't.

The Hammock

Here is the heaven
hung between pin oaks
and the blue water lapping,
and whatever's left
of a mid August evening
in your middle life.
This is the dozing
between waking and napping
the keening of loons
the hovering blue
of clouds in their heaven
the color that you
will always remember
when you remember.

This is the August
all those years back now
in Venice with your
Italian friend who taught
you the meagremost
bits of the language
enough to get by on
mia cara, mio tesoro
sei la piu bella del mondo
facciamo l'amore
ora adesso . . . here and now,

and the dream into which
you will often lapse
of the woman you loved then
so far removed,
and the fear that you felt
over drinks in the piazza
that she would be gone when
you returned.

And this is the moment
you will always return to—
not Venice nor August
but somewhere between
when, stopping for something
to drink and directions,
the woman you meet there
says this is for you—
the moment relieved of both
vision and history
her body made lovely
with grief and desire
she offers you outright
whether waking or dreaming
"Here," she says, "now,"
again and again;
here is a pleasure
for give and for getting
for laughing and weeping
to have and to hold,
the gift only kept

between coming and going
the body hung
as it is, between heavens
beloved and blessed, outstretched,
open and aching and only
momentarily your own—
"here," she says, and "now"—a present.

II

*A nod should be given to customs that disappeared.
Puckle tells of a curious functionary, a sort of male
scapegoat called the "sin-eater." It was believed in some
places that by eating a loaf of bread and drinking a
bowl of beer over a corpse, and by accepting a six-
pence, a man was able to take unto himself the sins of
the deceased whose ghost thereafter would no longer
wander.*

—Habenstein & Lamers,
The History of American Funeral Directing, 1955

Liberty

Some nights I go out and piss on the front lawn
as a form of freedom—liberty from
porcelain and plumbing and the Great Beyond
beyond the toilet and the sewage works.
Here is the statement I am trying to make:
to say I am from a fierce bloodline of men
who made their water in the old way, under stars
that overarched the North Atlantic where
the River Shannon empties into sea.
The ex-wife used to say, "Why can't you pee
in concert with the most of humankind
who do their business tidily indoors?"
It was gentility or envy, I suppose,
because I could do it anywhere, and do
whenever I begin to feel encumbered.
Still, there is nothing, here in the suburbs,
as dense as the darkness in West Clare
nor any equivalent to the nightlong wind
that rattles in the hedgerow of whitethorn there
on the east side of the cottage yard in Moveen.
It was market day in Kilrush, years ago:
my great-great-grandfather bargained with tinkers
who claimed it was whitethorn that Christ's crown was made from.
So he gave them two and six and brought them home—
mere saplings then—as a gift for the missus,
who planted them between the house and garden.

For years now, men have slipped out the back door
during wakes or wedding feasts or nights of song
to pay their homage to the holy trees
and, looking up into that vast firmament,
consider liberty in that last townland where
they have no crowns, no crappers and no ex-wives.

Argyle's Ejaculations

Argyle's preference in sins was legend.
The best of them were those the priest invented:
broken fasts or abstinence in Lent,
a tithe unpaid or Sunday morning passed
in honest, gainful labor or in bed.
He feasted full on Easter Duties missed
or some bad-mouthing of a Jesuit.
He relished churchy sins that had no flesh
or blood or bones, but only upset
some curate's dictum on moral etiquette
"God Bless His Holiness in Rome O Lord!"—
Argyle often ejaculated—
"And all Right Reverend Eminence & Graces,
and all the idle time thy have to kill
concocting new sins for my evening meal."
But then he'd dream that girl-child again,
defiled by some mannish violence who threw
herself to death, despairing, down a bog hole.
And when the parish house refused her requiems
her people sent for Argyle to come
and undo by his dinner what the girl had done.
But Argyle knelt and wept and refused the bread
and poured the bowl of bitters on the ground
and prayed "God spare my hunger till that churchman's dead."

Argyle in Carrigaholt

At Carrigaholt the priest was famous for
the loud abhorrence that he preached against
adherence to the ancient superstitions.
Old cures, evil eyes and hocus-pocuses
were banned as unholy forms of competition.
"The divil" he'd say, then something Latin
the townsmen took to mean *anathema,*
whenever the tinkers turned up in their wagons
full of charms and spells and red-haired daughters
telling fortunes and selling talismans.
Argyle got there quite by accident—
a wrong turn on the coastal road en route
to Loop Head where a sinner lay stone-dead
by dint of the eighty-some-odd years he'd lived
on that peninsula. But when the priest got wind
of it, he sent his acolytes to bring
the sin-eater in for inquisitioning.
And Argyle humored him all night until
the priest made threats of holy violence,
to which Argyle, grinning, said "Good priest, relent.
You do a brisk trade in indulgences
and tithes and votive lamps and requiems.
You keep your pope and robes and host and chalice.
Leave me my loaf and bowl and taste for malice."

Argyle's Retreat

Great hosts of basking sharks and shoals of mackerel,
like brethren in the one Creation, swam
together in the seas around Loop Head Point,
free of those long-standing habits of predation
whereby the larger fellow eats the small.
In Kilkee church, two girls saw statues move.
Lights appeared and disappeared and reappeared
from Doonaghboy to Newtown, and the dead were seen
perched upon ditchbanks with their turnip lamps by night.
In Moveen, cattle sang, crows barked and kittens flew
The tidal pools at Goleen filled with blood
and all the common wisdoms were undone
by signs and wonders everywhere. Argyle
wondered were they miracles or omens?—
God's handiwork or some bedevilment
called up or down on him by that avenging priest
he'd lately tangled with? Either way, *retreat*
was the word formed in him. A fortnight's rest
at Dingle, fast and prayer to purge and cleanse himself
among those holy hermits there who never
once, for all their vast privations, ever
saw or heard a thing or apprehended God
abounding in their stars or stones or seas
and, for all they had not witnessed, yet believed.

Argyle's Dream of the Churchdove

Argyle saw the Inner Hebrides
in dreams and dozings, spasms of the light
in which the vision under eyelids brightened
the dark precincts of ancient memory:
Iona in his father's father's time . . .
His father's father singing to the sea
a lamentation of his own mad making
aside the strand where blessed Columcille
first landed with his boats and brother monks
and looking back for Ulster couldn't see
beyond the thickening pale of exile.
O ancient gray eyed saint—the old one sang—
old sire of my bastard lineage,
please intercede with God to send a Sign
that I might know my bilious ministry
serves both the sinner and The Sinned Against.
At that a churchdove flew out of the fog
and striving skyward, shat upon his head,
the bird's anointing oozing into each
and every sensing orifice he had.
And shaken by the vision, Argyle,
uncertain of its meaning, nonetheless,
woke mouthing words of praise and wonderment
in fiery tongues, remarkable and strange.

Argyle's Return to the Holy Island

After the dream of the churchdove and the tongues,
Argyle contemplated pilgrimage
to that blessed island in the Hebrides
from which his ancient lineage had sprung
from the sainted loinage of Columbans,
whose couplings with the island women left
a legacy of zealotry, God-hunger,
genius and the occasional idiot
that worked its way down blighted centuries
of monks and anchorites and sin-eaters—
a race of men much gifted with their mouths
for giving out with prayers and poetry
or, like Argyle, for the eating of
sinful excess, shortfalls, mediocrities,
such as would set most lesser men to vomiting.
With neither mule nor map, Argyle walked
aimlessly throughout the western places
until he came to water which he crossed
from island to smaller island praising
the fierce weather, the full moon, the faithful boatman.
What makes this aching in the soul? he thought,
for distant islands where the silence hordes
the voices of our dead among the stones?
And though no answer was forthcoming, he went forth.

The Moveen Notebook

In memory of Nora Lynch

(1902–1992)

When I first came, the old dog barked me back,
all fang and bristle and feigned attack.
I stood frozen in the road. The taxi man,
counting his crisp punt notes from Shannon said,
"Go on boy. That's your people now." I went.
Sambo, the dog, went quiet as a bluff called.
Curtains parted in the house across the road.
The momentary sun gave way to rain.
3 *February* 1970—
the oval welcome in my first passport.
What kind of Yank comes in the dead of winter?
Nora stood in the doorway, figuring.

My grandfather's grandfather, Patrick Lynch—
her father's father, thus, our common man—
was given this cottage as a wedding gift
when he first brought Honora Curry here
from somewhere eastern of Kilrush. Well met,
I imagine, at a cattle mart
or ceilidh dance or kinsman's wedding;
and she the grandniece of Eugene O'Curry
whose name's on the college in Carrigaholt,
accounting, according to Nora, for
any latter genius in the gene pool.
"The O'Curry breed" she would always call it
when the answer was clever, or the correct one.

———

As for the newlyweds, they made children:
birthed a sickly daughter and five sons here
in the first spare decade after the famines.
The names repeat themselves down generations now of
Mary Ellens, Michaels, Sinons, Dans, Pats, Toms.
And pity little: what I know of them.

Michael, the eldest boy, impregnated
one of the McMahons from across the road.
(Maybe an aunt or grandaunt of old John Joe
who was aged when I first came here. He's dead
the Lord've mercy on him, ten years now.)
But Michael and his pregnant neighbor wed
and moved beyond the range of gossip here
and prospered and were happy it is said
in spite of the shame of that beginning.
And Dan died young and Mary Ellen, swept
from the ledgerocks at Doonlicky by
a freak wave when they were picking sea grass
to green the haggards with. As for Pat, the son,
he sailed to Melbourne and was never heard from
except for the tail end of a story of how
he sang from one end of the voyage
to another. "But for Lynch, we'd all do!"
it's said was said about him, his lovely tenor.
And Sinon married Mary Cunningham
and stayed here in the land—the first freehold
after centuries of British landlords.
And after Sinon died, 'twas Nora sold
eggs and new potatoes till the debt was paid

and kept her widowed mother into her age
and thereby let her own chances grow cold
for a life of men and motherhood. She stayed.
And her brother Tommy stayed and worked the land—
the loyal if withered and spinsterly end
of the line until, as Nora said, I came.

My great-grandfather sailed for Michigan—
Tomas O'Loinsigh, Nora's Uncle Tom—
and married Ellen Ryan there and worked
as a guard at Jackson Prison, pin-striped
Studebakers and lied about his age
for the warden or the factory boss or wife.
The parish house in Clare records his baptism
in 1861. The stone in Jackson's cut
1870. Either way, he died
in 1930 of the heart attack
that killed his son and killed my father after that.
And Nora, twisting these relations round once said:
"'Twas Tom that went and Tom that would come back."

All of which might seem unnecessary now
at the end of yet another century
on the brink of this brand-new millennium
trying to set these lives and times into
Life and Time in the much larger sense:
those ineluctable modalities
that joyous man said we were given to:
how we repeat ourselves, like stars in the dark night,
and after Darwin, Freud and popes and worlds at war,

we are still our father's sons and daughters
still our mother's darling girls and boys,
aging first, then aged then ageless.
We bury our dead and then become them.

What kind comes in the dead of winter then?
The kind that keeps a record, names names
says what happened, remembers certain things,
wakes the dead, leaves a witness for them after him.

So gospel or gossip, chitchat or my party piece:
a gift for my children, if they want it, this
membrance of the visit and revisiting
the stones, the fire, and the sod from which
we came, somehow, and must return again.

That first month in Moveen was wet and cold;
a fire on the floor, the open hearth,
the turf reddening against the wind that roared
up unencumbered out of Goleen bay.
And warmed likewise against the rising damp—
that pelting daylong nightlong driven rain
that fed the puddle underneath the land.
Nora hung huge pots and kettles from the crane
and settled them into the fire coals
to boil chicken, cabbage, potatoes
or bake the soda bread or steep the tea.
Or boil water for the cow that calved,
or mare that foaled or whatever hatched
in what seemed to me endless nativity

presided over by my distant cousins:
the chaste and childless aging siblings
Tommy and Nora Lynch of Moveen West
County Clare, "on the banks of the Shannon"
my grandfather always told us—"don't forget"—
after grace was said over turkey dinners.

Tommy died in March of seventy-one.
I still can see him laid out in his bed
a rosary laced among his fingers, thumbs
curled, the purple shroud, bright coppers on his eyelids,
the Missal propped between his chest and chin
as if to keep your man from giving out
with whatever the dead know that the living don't—
a tidy West Clare corpse in readiness.
Sean Collins brought the oaken coffin in
and Sonny Carmody and J. J. McMahon
and Sergeant and Tommy Hedderman
bore him on their shoulders through the yard
and out into the road where Collins' funeral car
waited with the neighbors' cars lined up behind it.
To Carrigaholt then into the cold church
where Fr. Duffy waited with his beads
and gave poor Tommy one glorious mystery
before returning to his tea and paper work.
Next morning, Mass, then down to Pearce Fennel's
where boozy eulogists recalled the way
that Tommy would stand among his cattle
and speak to them. He called them by their names.
Or how he sang "The Boys of Kilmichael"

whenever his turn came around those nights
of talk and song and dance and old stories,
more common in the townlands years ago.
And then the slow cortege to Moyarta
beneath sufficient rain to make us quote:
"Happy is the grave the rain falls on," of course
a paltry omen in those soggy parishes.
And he was buried there among the stones,
illegible with weather, worn by wind,
his mother's bones, his brother Mikey's bones—
a tidy pile beside the grave's backfill—
together again, interred, commingled,
on the banks of the River Shannon. "Don't forget."

Thus, "don't forget" becomes the prayer we pray
against the moment of our leave-taking—
the whispered pleadings to our intimates,
the infant held, the lover after lovemaking,
the child who ages, the elder who
returns to childhood again. "Gone west"
is what the Clare folks call it when some old
client on the brink of dying sees
a long-dead mother in a daughter's eyes
or hears God's voice Himself in the free advice
some churchman mutters among final sacraments.
"Be stingy with the lord and the lord will be
stingy with you" is what Fr. Kenny said,
which was his careful way of putting forth
the theory that you get what you pay for.

———

So do the dead pray for remembrance as
the living do? Are these the voices that we hear
those Marchy darknesses when the whitethorn limbs
tick along the eves and window ledges?
Or the wind hums in chimneys overhead:
or whispers to us underneath the door,
old names, old stories, old bits of wisdom?

"All winter we watch the fire" Nora said.
"All summer we watch the sea." Then she would sit
for hours hunched over, elbows to knees,
warming the palms of her hands to the fire
smoking the cigarettes from the duty-free
shop in Kennedy I would always bring her.

"Whatever happened 'twas a freak wave took them,
above in Doonlicky and a grand fine day
and they were swept, all Lynches and O'Dea's
two out of this house—a boy and girl—
and one out of Carmody's house above—
an uncle I suppose of old Kant Lynch's.

And where was the God in that I wonder?"

Then rising up amid her wonderments
she'd look out westwards past the windowpane
past Sean Maloney's house gone derelict
in half a dozen winters of disuse
over hedgerow after hedgerow until her gaze

would fix on Newtown and P. J. Roche's lights
where the lap of land rose upwards to the sea.

"I wonder if there's anything at all.
I wonder if He hears us when we pray."

Then chilled by her inquiries she'd sit
to stir her coals and hum *Amazing Grace,*
or give out with the names she kept alive
in the cold heaven of her memory
that tallied all but ten years of the century
the rest of us kept track of by the wars
but Nora measured by the ones she'd known:
who'd lived where, who'd married whom, who died.
And after that, who was left to grieve them.
Who waited in the land, who moved away.
Who sent home dollars. Who sent home pounds.
Who sang, who danced, who played, who drank too much.
"The cross off of an ass!" is what she'd say.
Who could be trusted, who couldn't be, who lied,
and who, though dead and buried still survived
in the talk of men in public houses
or the talk of women in shops and market stalls
or the talk of neighbors at stoves or fires:
the mention of the name that keeps the name alive
and what it was they did or didn't do
to win the race or save the day or just survive—
the extraordinary moment we attribute to
them alone, irrevocably. Them only.

———

As, for example, how Mary Maloney,
once kicked by a cow when she was a child
would work circles well around any man,
the limp notwithstanding. Or how she smiled.
Or the way her eyes unfailingly moistened
whenever she spoke of her dead mother.
Or how her brother Sean danced like a bull—
wide eyed and red faced when the music played.
Or how Dan Gorman, the Lord have mercy,
was mad for the drink and games of chance.
Or the way Kant Lynch's blinded eye
bore through me when I told him how I had
nearly been swept off the cliff at Doonlicky
by a wave that came up from the rocks behind—
a freak wave really like the hand of God—
that knocked me flat out inches from the edge.
"Mind yourself now boy," the old man said,
"the sea's ever hungry for Lynches there."
I can still see it now, near thirty years since—
the milky cataract, the thick brow arched,
the slim red warning in his good eye's squint.

As I see Johnny Hickey with his fiddle and
Denny Tubridy and his tin-whistle and
the pink Collins sisters, Bridie and Mae,
swooning in the corner to the music made
or that song Ann and Lourda Carmody sang—
Dow-n by th-e Sal-l-y gar-dens
M-y love a-nd I did meet . . .
when they were little more than little girls

singing of true romance before their time
for their elders whose moments had come and gone:
Maloneys and Murrays, Deloughreys and Downeses,
McMahons and Carmodys, Curtins and Keanes,
Burnses and Clancys, Walshes and Lynches—
old names that fit like hand-me-downs: too loose
at times, at times too snug, sometimes all too well
Like Theresa Murray and her sister Anne,
good neighbors who would call in on their rounds
to trade the current news, the talk in town
for Nora's ancient recollections of
the dead, the dying and the grown or gone.

And I see Nora in the years I know her
astride her Raleigh bike enroute to town,
(One time an old dog, barking, knocked her down.
She wore the cast a week then cut it off and
holding her hand up for inspection scoffed
"That wrist is right as paint. Three weeks? I'm healed.")
or walking with me up the coast road to
fish the mackerel or take the air or
ponder the imponderable expanse—
No parish between here and America.
We'd walk back then, with fresh fish and hunger.
Or how she battled with the Land Commission
to keep her thirty-acre heritage,
when certain neighbors had put in for it.
"Grabbers," she called them. "They want it for nothing."

———

"A cousin in America," she wrote
"a young and able man is coming soon"
ten months before this unknown cousin showed
up—twenty-ish, unwittingly, a sign from God.
No farmer, still, I kept it in the courts
for twenty years and Nora let the land
to P. J. Roche, from Newtown, a young man
with a wife and child and a resemblance to
Tommy, the brother who had died before.
And once over pints in Mary Hickie's bar
P.J. asked me would I ever sell, if
God forbid, something should ever happen.
Take care of Nora is the thing I told him,
and I'll take care of you. The deal was cut.
So that reoccurring dream I'd always had
of Nora dying some night in the dark,
alone, unmissed by anyone for days,
was put to rest. P.J. and Breda kept their part
and doted over Nora like their own.
I often thought of P.J.'s evenings there—
after saving hay or dosing cattle
or maybe on the way home from the bar
he'd stop for tea, she'd put down the kettle.
He'd organize himself then go home to Breda.
And knowing how it was, I envied that—
the quiet in the room, the way the light
went golden just before it died. The tune
she seemed always on the brink of singing,
the tiny rattle of the cups and saucers dried,
the talk between a young man and a fierce old woman.

———

And Nora outlived the Land Commission
and most of those who'd tried to take her land.
(One was found, fell off his tractor in a ditch
and no few thought that maybe Nora's ban
was the thing that brought him to that hapless end.)
Two weeks before she died I had her will
the land outright to P.J. and his wife.
I kept the house, the haggards, and the yards,
I kept the cow-cabins, out-offices,
I kept her name in Moveen where it'd been
as far back as anyone remembered,
because I think that's what she had in mind.
And I dream you, my darling Nora, now
free of great stone vault at Moyarta
restored to the soft chair by the fire,
a kettle on, the kitten sleeping still
among the papers on the window ledge
and, maybe April, the one you never
lived to see, greening out of doors. And we
are talking in the old way, talking still,
of how the cuckoo's due here any day,
or how to count the magpies for a sign.
"A great life if you do not weaken!
And if you do . . . " you say. You turn and smile.

You approve of the hearth I had your P.J. build
of smooth gray stones drawn up from Shannonside
and how the flagstone floor was raised and thick
dampcourse put down and sand poured under it,
a window opened in the northern side,

the bathroom tiled like a French bordello
and every wall repainted *apricot*
on Mrs. Carmody's own good counsel.
You approve, likewise, of how I stir the coals
and add the sods and stare into the fire.

Is what I see there what makes me reckon
the lives we live in counterclockwise turns,
better at elegy than commencement,
better at what was done than what's to do?
To bury the dead must we first unearth them,
to see the bones still brittle in the dust,
the poor kite-work on which the poorer flesh
was hung? Is it afterwards their voices
return to us in the words of others?
In the call of blackbirds or the noise of
wind and rainfall at the window sash?
Is it in their silence that the noisome
truth is spoken, the body's hunger hushed,
as last night's reddened coals turn whitened ash?
Is not the grave's first utterance, "enough, enough"?

An Evening Walk to the Sea by Friesians

So much in this place comes in black and white—
the cattle and clergy, magpies, the stars and dark,
those crisp arithmetics for how things are:
one for sorrow, two for joy, three to marry, four, five . . .
or the tally of Shalts and Thou Shalt Nots.
Despite the stars' vast evidence, we count.

A score of Michael Murray's Friesian calves
lift their faces from their pasturage
to stand and watch me standing, watching back,
my stillness and their stillness counterbalancing.
I'm making for the cliffs to fish for mackerel
to share with neighbors over evening tea.

And on these yearling hides, like seas and continents,
a random mapwork that yet articulates
a world of hard borders, sharp opposites,
clear options where the right is manifest,
the kindly husbandry of what is obvious.
Suspect of certainties, I watch the tides—

———

their comings and their goings, rise and fall,
the edges of approach and leave-taking
in constant motion, changing constantly
the division of ocean and landfall.
Likewise the evening light, likewise the line
between the seascape and the darkening sky

where mountains or cloudbanks or maybe islands blur
into a frontier without horizons.
God's Will, like anyone's guess at the weather,
the count we keep of certain birds, the firmament,
bright fish, the cows in their now distant fields, astray:
whatever comes in black and white goes gray.

Bishop's Island

Two holy men came out here long ago
and prayed against the ground that bound them to
the green mainland and their prayers were answered.
Thus, from their rock in the North Atlantic
they watched for God among such signs and wonders
as sea and sky and wind and dark supply:
fury and firmament and privations
enough to dull the flesh, and beauty too,
to break the heart. They wept with gratitude,
kept silent, built an oratory. There,
you can see the ruins of it from the coast road.
Seabirds brought them mackerel it is said.
Fresh water sprung from the rock. When one died
the other buried him and cut a stone
then died himself some few years after that.
And everything was swept—his hut, his bones—
into the vast ocean and was forgot
until some bishop on a pilgrimage
centuries later, as bishops often did,
declared them saints, proclaimed the holy island His.

Report from Ballylee to the Dead Master

Gray, bloodshot men still stand on corners, waiting
or lean in shop windows and twitch their heads
in mum consensus with the passers-by:
Indeed! *What shall we do with this absurdity?*
Old women, bent from cold or widowhood
still go to town for messages, for tea and bread
the bit of rasher for tomorrow morning,
for news of the newly dead and halves of Paddy.
School girls still walk arm in arm in blue gymslips
or green ones, neckties and anklets, white blouses—
bright novices before their final vows.
Boys still leave for England or America.
This is no country for young men, either.
This morning I drove from Shannon through Ballylee
to get your benediction on the work I do
in the latter years of this, your century.
You knew this place. I borrow it from you.
Just as I've borrowed other voices here:
the bitter spinster spitting in her coals
mumbling "Bollocks" and "Dead Loss," cursing her neighbors;
the publican with his easy answers,
the curate in his cups and catechism
holding forth with Ways and Truths and Lights,
the daft tin-whistler thumping his bootheels
to keep the concertina man in step—
the gladsong of a place grown wary of

old heroes, histories and politics.
Sixty years since you, you'd know it still—
O heart, O troubled heart—this caricature:
They've done the roof this year. Your tower stands.
Ruin is a slow business. Your characters remain.

Byzance

He gave his wife the scent that woman wore
he'd met once in the lounge-bar of the Gresham
and later took up to the suite of rooms
that overlooked the Pro-Cathedral dome
and traded mouths and hands and wetness with
then held well into the next mid-morning.

Coffee at Bewley's, lunch at Powerscourt,
they went their separate ways then with a wave—
moments only in each other's histories.
Whenever she wears that fragrance now, he is
transformed, transported, momentarily
restored to the penthouse of the Gresham:

She sits in her bright flesh at the vanity
touching herself behind her ears, between
her breasts, under her knees. She rubs her wrists
together. Pulse points she calls them, smiling.
Someone has left them mints on the pillows,
kindled the fire, turned the bedlinens down.

Aisling

Whenever he left her
there was always a landscape
into which he would bring her
in her linen dress
to circle a fir tree
where black birds were nesting
in the first green field
beyond the formal gardens.
He would sit at the big desk
in the bay window
in the west room they'd given him
to do it in.
He would try to describe it—
the shape of her turning
and the tune she was humming
and the way she drew
the hem of her dress up
with her small arms rising
and falling and rising
in a kind of flight.
He would try to decide if
later, by evening,
when the light was behind her
if she really knew
how the lines of her body
sharpened by twilight

would step from her clothing
in a silhouette,
if she knew how it filled him
with grief and desire
watching the gardens
and the green go black
while birds in the fir tree
settled into silence
and the great bay window
darkened where he sat—
a dark so black
he could never, ever
let her into it.

Moyarta

When Patrick Lynch's wife Honora died
a century ago, he built this vault,
so keen was his bereavement only stone

would dull it. He drew slates down by the cartload
from the coast road in Moveen with which he built
the deep walls and the taller gabled end

to stand against the rush of rain and wind
that garbled oven continents in stone.
Smooth gray rocks from the Shannon were drawn up

to make the floor, to set her coffin on
and down from Liscannor by turns he brought
the mighty ledger flag, eight foot by four,

on which Mick Troy from Kilballyowen,
the famous stonecutter from out the west,
cut deep these words that Pat had given him:

Erected by Pat Lynch in memory
of his beloved wife Honora Lynch
alias Curry. Died October 3rd

1889 aged 62 years.
May she R.I.P. IHS Amen.
All that's there still. You may go and see it.

Rentals Ledger

Des Kenny up in Galway made this book
of pages fit for ink and acid-free
and sewn into a leather binding. He
put *Lynch—Moveen West* on the cover. Look
there's white space left for the likes of you.
So if you're a writer the rent is *do*.
Pay Breda Roche coin of the realm for coal
and turf, fresh linens, clean towels. The phone's
on the honor system. Pay as you go.
But leave this absentee landlord poems,
paragraphs, sentences, phrases well turned
out of your own word horde and what you've learned.
Or better still, out of the stillness—what you hear
here in these ancient remedial stones
where Nora Lynch held forth for ninety years,
the last two decades of them on her own.
Alone by the fire in the silence she
recited the everyday mysteries
of wind and rain and darkness and the light
and sang her evening songs and sat up nights
full of wonder and reminiscences.
If you hear voices here the voice is hers.
She speaks to me still. If she speaks to you,
ready your best nib. Write what she tells you to.

The Old Operating Theatre, London,
All Souls Night

To rooms like this old resurrectionists
returned the bodies they had disinterred—
fresh corpses so fledgling anatomists
could study Origin & Insertion points
of deltoids, pecs, trapezius and count
the vertebrae, the ball & socket joints.
And learn the private parts and Latin names
by which the heart becomes a myocardium,
the high cheek bone a zygoma, the brain,
less prone to daydream as a cerebellum.

And squirming in their stiff, unflinching seats,
apprentice surgeons witnessed, in the round,
new methods in advanced colostomy,
the amputation of gangrenous limbs
and watched as Viennese lobotomists
banished the ravings of a raving man
but left him scarred and drooling in a way
that made them wonder was he much improved?
But here the bloodied masters taught dispassionate
incisions—how to suture and remove.

In rooms like this, the Greeks and Romans staged
their early dramas. Early Christians knelt
and hummed their liturgies when it was held
that prayer and penance were the only potions.

Ever since Abraham, guided by God,
first told his tribesmen of the deal he'd made—
their foreskins for that ancient Covenant—
good medicine's meant letting human blood.
Good props include the table and the blade.
Good theatre is knowing where to cut.

St. James' Park Epistle

I

To whom should this be
tendered then?
What hapless addressee

among old friends,
acquaintances, extended
family?

Or maybe former lovers?
First or last or best
among

the company of *Dear X*'s,
lost darlings, fond
regrets

or, failing these, maybe
Dear Sir or Madam?
Better yet

a packet left for strangers
without postage
or return

for one and all or
any, thus:
To whom it may concern.

II

Eventually
the French girls
and the waterfowl bend

outside of memory.
What's ever left
after the blue

morning, the trees blooming,
Her Majesty's
formal gardens

busy with the
blessed and elect
are but impressions—

bits of pigment only,
dots of light
assembled and then

reassembled
to amount to
something that resembles

this life, this
morning in the park, this
April, this London.

You can see the
oil on canvas
and the watercolor

versions of this metaphor
hung on walls
not far from here

at the Tate or
V & A or
National Gallery.

Or sit and watch with me here
on a bench. Here,
take a seat

beside the water,
among these ancient
flowering trees

whilst European
tourists, the Yanks
and Japanese

and brightly
colored subjects of the
former Empire

late millennial members
of the various
species

go by in bunches.
Sit back. Squint
so that the image blurs

until it all comes clear
and you have
all but disappeared

among the crowded
present tense and
one dimensional.

III

Oh my heart's friend
there is so much
I would like to tell you.

So much I have forgotten
So much more
I thought I knew.

A brief of easy wisdoms,
lessons learned,
then lost again.

Age is spillage,
memory the residue.
Life is death

kept at an arm's length.
Love is grief
dressed in its Sunday best.

And sadness is the tax
assessed on
any happiness.

Forgive me.
I go on a bit.
Maybe it comes with age.

I tend towards preachment
and the body politic.
I rage.

When all I ever wanted
was to offer
a witness—

to say
this is how it was and
this is how it wasn't.

Every effort to
live in the minute
is undone.

IV

The day itself
I am obliged to tell you
will be gone.

In spite of all our
efforts at remembrance,
still, they go.

The golden light,
the bright greensward,
these gifts are seasonal.

Crocus and daffodil
lilac, magnolia
tulip, rose,

the lilting songbirds
fly, alight and
sing and leave again

to join that company
of things that came
and were and went

that populate our heavens,
El Dorados,
the abyss,

on either side
of this blink in the eye
we give a name

and figure dates
to add and subtract from
the nothingness.

V

Those mothers with babies,
old men with dogs,
each one's possessed

of its own un-
doing, the seedling
of its taking leave

by growth or withering
love or love's grief,
the grave's dull math:

What blooms dries.
What sings goes silent.
What is will cease to be.

Try as you might to hold
those two embracing
there, they leave—

taking their true loves,
their quiet hungers,
hearts' desires

the bright moment
glistening only
momentarily

their little histories
intersecting oh so
briefly

possessed for the time
being of only
the time being.

VI

And so it always is,
after a life or
a half-life

we keep neither
the morning nor the
memory of it

intact and undisturbed.
The hearts' archives
are mostly

empty. Mostly
open, mostly full of
echoes only

of those moments
when the soul winced
or the heart spilled over

or the body
like a river overran
its borders

into the eager
dear aching embrace
of another.

Oh, we keep the icons,
room keys, matchbooks,
snapshots, coasters;

we save the programs
and the ticket stubs,
the souvenirs;

we press the roses
nosegays, bouquets,
withered boutonnieres

between the pages of
a kind of diary
we keep

that's mostly white space,
borders, bits and
pieces, potpourri

of dim details,
maybe the mention
of the place, maybe

the way his or her
body felt against
your body—

the taste of it, touch
of it, the utterly
otherness,

the urgent affirmations,
sweet nothings,
love's utterance:

some talk of the weather
and music
if there was music,

the slow progress of hands
and fingers lingering
Oh yes

just there and lips
that press and part
and open to a kiss

and kissing in return
return to this:
what you wore then

what was on the menu,
what was said or what
wasn't said

that made you want to get
naked and taken
or given

something absolute
by another of
your kind, something

lovely and opposite
that fit precisely
your hunger.

VII

After everything
there's so little to
remember.

The lovely
undulant conduct
of love between humans,

the passionate traffic in
comfort and
comisery.

There is so much to lose:
the slow touch of
your beloved,

the voice of your mother,
your father's eyes,
your child's hands,

the faces of brothers and sisters
the names of
old friends,

the company of perfect
strangers, the
news of the world.

VIII

The city of the dead
is rising round us
everywhere

The gray stone towers,
the bridges over the
gray river,

the record of mean time
rung out on
the quarter hour.

Remembrance is the green
space in the busy
cityscape.

The young go by
in various embraces.
The elders

memorize the names of things,
the flora and
the fauna

kings and queens,
old heroes cut in stone
and statuary.

But memory is the
ever changing image
that is found,

when pausing on the small
footbridge we
stare into the pond

and there the moment
hesitates but
momentarily

between the telling
how it was and
how it yet will be.

III

Love is like a stove. It burns you when it's hot. Love hurts.
—words & music by Boudleaux Bryant as sung by Roy Orbison

A Rhetoric upon Brother Michael's Rhetoric upon the Window

Like you, I wonder why the face of God
is any more hidden from us than a neighbor's
beaming over the back fence with his gab
and gossip. Why all this cloak-and-dagger
ritual of blood, these scriptural intrigues,
these hocus-pocuses, hide-and-seeks
by which the blind are given leave to lead the blind.
And you, out in Arkansas with your wife
and boys and bosom friends who drop around
to keep that vigil with you that you keep
at the window, waiting for a Sign.
You say you're waiting for a bird this time?
A hummingbird, no less, its wings a-blur
with furious deity, to appear
in all its majesty and take you up
into that rapture where the light is blue
and you become a hummingbird yourself.
Whereupon you pose the Eternal Question:
what if after that there's only space
and silence, once the hummingbirds are through—
the bright vision vanished without a trace?
What if, after everything, there's only you
and your imagination of that light?
What if we find that image and likeness
gazing back at us behind the eyes
of our darling sons and daughters or the eyes

in the faces of women we sleep with
or the timely friend with time to kill enough
to listen to us while we spill our guts
about our latest heartbreak or our sins?
What if the window is for looking in—
where we abide with our personal saviors
who save us from ourselves? Are they gods enough?
The lovers and children and the heart's neighbors
who turn the words to flesh and dwell with us?

Loneliest of Trees, The Winter Oak

—after Housman

Loneliest of trees, the winter oak
Still leafy here in bald November
Though withered still whispers "Remember . . .
After All Hallows, All Saints, All Souls . . ."

Now of my three score years and ten
Fifty will not come again
And seventy autumns, less a score . . .
I'm only left with twenty more.

And since twenty winters aren't enough
To contemplate the taking of our leaves,
About the woods I'll go and gather such
Lessons as there are in fallen leaves.

One of Jack's

The body is that of a white female,
sixty-eight inches and ninety-six pounds
appearing well-developed and poorly
nourished and appearing consistent with
the stated age of thirty-nine years.
The body is cold with full rigor mortis
and posteriorly distributed
widespread fixed cherry red livor mortis.
The body is very emaciated
with loss of body fat and muscles.
The scalp hairs are brown and long. There is dried
vomitus on the face, around the mouth
and on the neck. Natural teeth are present.
The pupils are dilated. There are
no conjuctival petechiae or
hemorrhage. There is no visible injury
on face or head. The neck is without injury.
The chest is symmetrical. The breasts are small
and symmetrical. There are no palpable
masses in the breasts. The intercostal
spaces are retracted, making the rib
prominences visible. The abdomen
is scaphoid. Evidence of previous
surgery is present over the abdomen.
The genitalia are that of an adult
female type without injury or

abnormality. There is mild
edema over the legs and ankles.
The upper extremities and back are
unremarkable. There are two patches
on the upper back, one on either side.
On the right side the labeling on the patch
reads "100 mg/h Duragestk (Fentanyl)."
The patch on the left side has a hand-written note
indicating "9-30 Tuesday."
The index of the right hand has a small
white string which measures ten inches in length.
At the end of the string there is a metal clip.

Life as We Knew It

Neighbor couples and their designer dogs
go walking with leashes these bright mornings.
At every corner there are dangers, warnings.
At every intersection, options, wonders, signs.
At crossings the lesson is to mind the traffic.
They learn to speak and heel and fetch and to return.
The men in their stiff collars barking wisdoms.
They pose and sniff. They howl and growl and whine.
The wives and pets grow weary of listening.
Some things only the dogs hear. Some the women.

Bells and Whistles

The Presbyterian bells play
"Be Still My Soul." Out Commerce Rd.,
the Catholics toll the *Angelus*.
The monkish cross themselves and pray.
The fire whistle signals some
damage within earshot. Men drop
what they're doing, come on the run,
breakneck with their lights and sirens:
a housefire or heart attack,
or else news of a child lost
or grim word of a child found.
In life, we sing, we are in death.

Heavenward

Such power in the naming of things—
to walk out in the greensward pronouncing
goldfinch, lilac, oriental poppy—
as if the shaping of the thing in sound
produced a pleasure like the sight of things
as if *the housefinch winters in the mock-orange* is
as tasty an intelligence to the lips and ears as
the sight of a small purple bird in December is
perched in a thicket of bald branches.
June you remember: *the white blossoms, yellow
jackets, the fresh scent of heaven.*
And other incarnations to be named:
nuthatch, magnolia, coreopsis, rose.
Surely this was God's first gift of godliness—
that new index finger working over the globe
assigning from the noisy void those fresh,
orderly syllables. *Ocean, garden,
helpmate, tree of knowledge.*
Making came easy, creation
a breeze. But oh, that dizzy pleasure when
God said *Eve* and the woman looked heavenward.

West Highland

Whenever I hear their aged names—
Lena, Cora Mae, Lydia, Bea—
I think of prim, widowed ladies from
the Baptist Church in West Highland Township;
and imagine their ordered, born-again lives
beyond the latter-day suburban sprawl
of disenchantment and convenience stores.
Lives lived out at the same pace as their mothers
and their mothers' people years before them,
between potlucks and bake sales and bazaars,
missions and revivals, Sunday to Sunday.
And for romance, they had Nights to Remember—
in summer, the Bible School picnics,
October, the Farm Bureau Harvest Ball.
All winter long, they courted in parlors
with men named Thurmond or Wilbur or Russell Lloyd.
They married at Easter and bore children
and outlived their husbands and tend the graves now
after Sunday services, weather permitting.
Whenever I see them, arm in arm,
at funerals where they sing or bring baked hams
in memory of one of their sisters, dead
of the long years or the nursing home,
I think of how the century for them
was neither wars nor science nor the evening news
but a blur of careful rites of passage:

baptisms and marriages and burials.
And I envy their heavens furnished like parlors
with crocheted doilies on the davenport
and Aunt Cecelia, who never got married,
singing "In the Garden" or "Abide with Me"
and God the Father nodding in His armchair
at saints and angels who come and go
with faces like neighbors and with names they know.

November

So he sits, the cranky bastard,
all wind and discontent
pissing and moaning out
his litany of missed chances.
The seasonal miscellany:
distemper and contempt.
These sadnesses, outrages, each
bleak utterance eleven times
more dire than the one before:
all overripened versions of
promise, the possible, hope, love.

Whenever she visits
he's on best behavior.
He eats what she brings him
and tries not to drool. She hugs him—
all bone and damp and chill.
The darkness he nods into leaves
a thin horizon—a
wince or grin?—she can never say.
An old dream of beauty? Heartbreak?
Something he's eaten? She gives thanks,
kisses his head, gone bald now, leaves.

Tongue and Groove

They meet in a movie
in which she stars
as the one on the bottom.
He is the one on the top.
This goes on for what
seems a long time.
Then they swap
partners or positions or
pink body parts
all in an effort to achieve
a believable rhythm of delight.
Like tongue and groove
they fit their parts.
Still, life, after lights
camera and action,
affirms the sad proprieties.
None of it will ever happen:
the dinner by candlelight
they might imagine,
the intimate glances,
the talk until dawn.
She never goes out with
the men that she works with.
For all the same reasons
he seldom talks.
Never on the first date.

She Instructs the Brethren
on the Laws of Love

You are but one in a long line of rapists
or lovers. Eventually, she will forget
the names, the faces, the earnest promises,
foreplay and afterglow. She will remember this:
how it was always a question of whether to bathe first
or first call the cops in to save the evidence.

Here is the comfort: she does not mean to hurt you.
She will hardly press charges or hold a grudge.
But do not ask Why if, after you've made love,
she weeps quietly. It is not yours to know.
Do not take it personally. Roll over.
Go to sleep. It has nothing to do with you.

The Lives of Women

A water bucket in the birthing room
to drown the female babies in is how
they do it in the outer provinces.
In other places amniocentesis gives
fair warning to the swift abortionist.
They take the tiny fetuses away
in baskets to a retort in the basement.
The smoke their bodies burning makes is hardly noticed.
In overpeopled cities, fat man-children
waddle through the streets like little emperors.
Their skinny sisters, barefoot behind them,
rummage in their litter for the leftovers.
Any survivors are taken to market
arrayed in jewels and ornamental dress—
exotic packages. The men stroll through the stalls
nodding and smiling, haggling prices.
Here in the suburbs we do it with promises
of endless protection and acts of love.
We send them to good schools and make them our muses.
We send them to market with their credit cards,
glad in their fashions and their minivans.
We marry them. We call them by our names.
We do the dishes and help with the children.
We ask their opinions. We nod and smile.
We keep the buckets and the baskets hidden.

That Scream if You Ever Hear It

You know who you are you
itchy trigger-fingered sonovabitch
always at my elbow with your
"Rub their noses in it.
Give it to them raw.
Spare the cutesy metaphor and bullshit.
Say what it was you heard or saw without
one extra syllable."

How some biker with a buzz-on
doing eighty in a forty-five
broadsides a Buick
killing the babies buckled in the front seat
leaving the babies' mother with a limp,
a lengthy facial scar,
a scream stuck in her somewhere
north of her belly, south of her teeth.

I know you don't need symmetry or order
so that the biker died in pieces—
the arm with the tattoo reading SHIT
HAPPENS thrown a hundred yards from the one
with NO TOMORROW on it—doesn't impress you.

———

But here's a little truth
you will approve my telling of:
The mom is going to leave her husband
fight with her father,
curse the priest.
She is going to go and live in the city,
have her face fixed, drink too much,
begin to sleep around in search
of the one and only one who can
tickle that scream out of her.

Maybe you'll run into her.
Maybe you're the one.

Here's another thing you will appreciate.
I know you'll like this. Listen up:
That scream, if you ever hear it,
won't rhyme with anything.

Nuptials

Like geese in October
they honk through town
in rented suits and cars,
their nuptials
fresh in their ears as
their first coupling,
flesh to separate flesh,
proclaimed in private:
we are one now,
we may comfort,
succour and damage,
love and be fruitful.
They kiss in the backseat
of the limousine.
Black satin and white lace
they wave and smile.
We gawk from the sidewalks.
They are strangers to us.

The Riddance

In her memory of it
he had never harmed her.
For weeks after the burial
he'd been so sweet.
Slow and deliberate,
he had only touched her
for pleasure, her pleasure.
Attentive to detail,
tender as newlyweds
on a kind of honeymoon,
they conducted their
intimate business in
the breathless lexicons
of hope and forgiveness.
It was only after
the casseroles had been
returned, the borrowed chairs,
the children gone home
to their other lives,
the sister moved back to the
Midwest and the thank-you's
mailed out for all condolences,
that she sat in the chill parlor
of her new widowhood
remembering the bruises,

the boozy gropings
and sad truths. And hugging herself
in the quiet she reckoned
the riddance she held there
was a good one.

Tommy

He keeps trying to replicate that day
in late September on the Pere Marquette
when the salmon were running. How they bet
on the first fish and the most fish and the weight
of the biggest and the best. He was nine.
His mother and father were not divorced.
The salmon went upstream to spawn and die.
There seemed to be an order to the universe.
He has a picture of himself that day,
holding two cohos, looking capable.
Behind him trees are turning. It is autumn.
His mother is back home with Mike and Sean
and Heather, his sister, and all the while
his father keeps coaxing him: Smile! Smile!

Russ

Hot air balloons—
fat flaming birds
adrift in evening air—
put me in mind
of Russ, my giant
crazy neighbor,
daft and absolute,
prone to grand gestures,
dead now a year
who always said I should
scatter his ashes
down on his townspeople
from overhead
some August, he told me,
when they least expect it—
during Sidewalk Sales
or Old Homes Tour
or Milford Memories.

There There

He wanted to be the victim of something,
to get on a talk show and spill his guts
on just how it was he came to be this way—
the awful dysfunction of his upbringing
the sorry particulars of which he could make up
to fit the prime-time appetite for pain.
Just once he wanted the studio audience
to moan in disbelief on his behalf
and for Oprah to take his hand in her hand
and tell him There There Everything Will Be Alright.

Antilles

A profusion of humming-
birds and bougainvillea
whose abundant blooming
is no more the pleasure

than the sound of its saying
in your mouth—how it blooms
in lips and tongue and teeth
like the name for something

learned from a lover or
done with a stranger
or a gift borne home
after distant travel

for your beloved
who waves from the
front porch welcome and wooing
smiling down on you like bougainvillea.

These Things Happen
in the Lives of Women

The first time he ever bought her lingerie
she was dead of gin and librium and years
of trying to regain her innocence.
"These things happen in the lives of women . . ."
is what the priest told him. "They lose their way."
And lost is what she looked like lying there
awash in her own puke and the disarray
of old snapshots and pill bottles,
bedclothes and letters and momentos
of the ones with whom she had been intimate.
She was cold already. Her lips were blue.
So he bought her a casket and red roses
and bought silk panties and a camisole
and garters and nylons and a dressing gown
with appliqués in the shape of flowers.
And after the burial he bought a stone
with her name and dates on it and wept aloud
and went home after that and kept weeping.

Grimalkin

One of these days she will lie there and be dead.
I'll take her out back in a garbage bag
and bury her among my sons' canaries,
the ill-fated turtles, a pair of angelfish:
the tragic and mannerly household pests
that had the better sense to take their leaves
before their welcomes or my patience had worn thin.
For twelve long years I've suffered this damned cat
while Mike, my darling middle son, himself
twelve years this coming May, has grown into
the tender if quick-tempered manchild
his breeding blessed and cursed him to become.
And only his affection keeps this cat alive
though more than once I've threatened violence—
the brick and burlap in the river recompense
for mounds of furballs littering the house,
choking the vacuum cleaner, or what's worse:
shit in the closets, piss in the planters, mice
that winter indoors safely as she sleeps
curled about a table leg, vigilant
as any knickknack in a partial coma.
But Mike, of course, is blind to all of it—
the gray angora breed of arrogance,
the sluttish roar, the way she disappears for days
sex-desperate once or twice a year,
urgently ripping her way out the screen door

to have her way with anything that moves
while Mike sits up with tuna fish and worry,
crying into the darkness, "Here kitty kitty,"
mindless of her whorish treacheries
or of her crimes against upholsteries—
the sofas, love seats, wingbacks, easy chairs
she's puked and mauled into dilapidation.
I have this reoccurring dream of driving her
deep into the desert east of town
and dumping her out there with a few days' feed
and water. In the dream, she's always found
by kindly tribespeople who eat her kind
on certain holy days as a form of penance.
God knows, I don't know what he sees in her.
Sometimes he holds her like a child in his arms
rubbing her underside until she sounds
like one of those battery powered vibrators
folks claim to use for the ache in their shoulders.
And under Mike's protection she will fix her
indolent green-eyed gaze on me as if
to say: Whaddaya gonna do about it, Slick,
the child loves me and you love the child.
Truth told, I really ought to have her fixed
in the old way with an airtight alibi,
a bag of Redi-mix and no eyewitnesses.
But one of these days she will lie there and be dead.
And choking back loud hallelujahs, I'll pretend
a brief bereavement for my Michael's sake,
letting him think as he has often said
"Deep down inside you really love her don't you Dad?"

I'll even hold some cheerful obsequies
careful to observe God's never-failing care
for even these, the least of His creatures,
making some mention of a cat-heaven where
cat-ashes to ashes, cat-dust to dust
and the Lord gives and the Lord has taken away.
Thus claiming my innocence to the end,
I'll turn Mike homeward from that wicked little grave
and if he asks, we'll get another one because
all boys need practice in the arts of love
and all boys' aging fathers in the arts of rage.

How It's Done Here

We heat graves here for winter burials
as a kind of foreplay before digging in,
to soften the frosthold on the ground before
the sexton and his backhoe do the opening.
Even the earth resists our flesh in this weather—
regards the mess a new grave makes in snow
the way a schoolgirl in her new prom dress
regards defilement. It is over, though,
almost before it's started, almost routine.
The locals mount in their brisk procession,
the cleric with a few words of release
commits the body to its dispossession,
then blesses everyone, seen and unseen,
against forgetfulness and disbelief.

Iambs for the Day of Burial

Of all our private parts the heart knows best
that love and grieving share the one body
and keeps a steady iambic tally
of this life's syllables, stressed and unstressed.
Our pulse divided by our breathing equals
pleasure measured in pentameters,
pain endured in oddly rhyming pairs:
sadness, gladness, sex and death, nuptials,
funerals. Love made and love forsaken—
each leaves us breathless and beatified,
more than the sum of parts that lived and died
of love or grief. Both leave the heart broken.

At the Opening of Oak Grove
Cemetery Bridge

Before this bridge we took the long way around
up First Street to Commerce, then left at Main,
taking our black processions down through town
among storefronts declaring *Dollar Days!*
Going Out of Business! Final Mark Downs!
Then pausing for the light at Liberty,
we'd make for the Southside by the Main Street bridge
past used-car sales and party stores as if
the dead required one last shopping spree
to finish their unfinished business.
Then eastbound on Oakland by the jelly-works,
the landfill site and unmarked railroad tracks—
by bump and grinding motorcade we'd come
to bury our dead by the river at Oak Grove.

And it is not so much that shoppers gawked
or merchants carried on irreverently.
As many bowed their heads or paused or crossed
themselves against their own mortalities.
It's that bereavement is a cottage industry,
a private enterprise that takes in trade
long years of loving for long years of grief.
The heart cuts bargains in a marketplace
that opens after hours when the stores are dark
and Christmases and Sundays when the hard
currencies of void and absences

nickel-and-dime us into nights awake
with soured appetites and shaken faith
and a numb hush fallen on the premises.

Such stillness leaves us moving room by room
rummaging through cupboards and the closet space
for any remembrance of our dead lovers,
numbering our losses by the noise they made
at home—in basements tinkering with tools
or in steamy bathrooms where they sang in the shower,
in kitchens where they labored over stoves
or gossiped over coffee with the nextdoor neighbor,
in bedrooms where they made their tender moves;
whenever we miss that division of labor
whereby he washed, she dried; she dreams, he snores;
he does the storm windows, she does floors;
she nods in the rocker, he dozes on the couch;
he hammers a thumbnail, she says "Ouch!"

This bridge allows a residential route.
So now we take our dead by tidy homes
with fresh bedlinens hung in the backyards
and lanky boys in driveways shooting hoops
and gardens to turn and lawns for mowing
and young girls sunning in their bright new bodies.
First to Atlantic and down Mont-Eagle
to the marshy north bank of the Huron
where blue heron nest, rock bass and bluegill
bed in the shallows and life goes on.
And on the other side, the granite rows

of Johnsons, Jacksons, Ruggles, Wilsons, Smiths—
the common names we have in common with
this place, this river and these winter oaks.

And have, likewise in common, our own ends
that bristle in us when we cross this bridge—
the cancer or the cardiac arrest
or lapse of caution that will do us in.
Among these stones we find the binding thread:
old wars, old famines, whole families killed by flus,
a century and then some of our dead
this bridge restores our easy access to.
A river is a decent distance kept.
A graveyard is an old agreement made
between the living and the living who have died
that says we keep their names and dates alive.
This bridge connects our daily lives to them
and makes them, once our neighbors, neighbors once again.

The Nines

Thus we proclaim our fond affirmatives:
"I will, I do, Amen, Hear Hear! Let's
eat, drink and be merry." Marriage is
the public spectacle of private parts:
checkbooks and genitals, housewares, fainthearts,
all doubts becalmed by kissing aunts, a priest's
safe homily, those tinkling glasses
tightening those ties that truly bind
us together forever, dressed to the nines.

Darling, I reckon maybe thirty years,
given our ages and expectancies.
Barring the tragic or untimely, say,
ten thousand mornings, ten thousand evenings,
please God, ten thousand moistened nights like this,
when, mindless of these vows, our opposites,
nonetheless, attract. Thus, love's subtractions:
the timeless from the ordinary times—
nine thousand, nine hundred, ninety-nine.

Maura

She had never desired him in that way—
that aching in the skin she'd sometimes get
for a man possessed of that animal something.

Something outside of language or regret. No,
he'd been the regular husband, the hedged bet
against the bag lady and spinsterhood;

a cap on the toothpaste, the mowed lawn, bills paid;
a well-insured warm body in the bed,
the kindly touch if seldom kindling.

Odd, then, to have a grief so passionate
it woke her damp from dreams astraddle him—
the phantom embraced in pillows and blankets,

or sniffed among old shirts and bureau drawers.
She fairly swooned sometimes remembering
the curl of her name in his dull tenor.

Sweet nothings now rewhispered in her ears.
She chose black lace, black satin, reckoning
such pain a kind of romance in reverse.

The house filled with flowers. She ate nothing.
Giddy and sleepless, she longed for him alone.
Alone at last, she felt a girl again.

In the Garden

St. Francis in Frank Caswell's garden stands
watch over hostas and daylilies and
Frank's dead wife's cremated remains, planted

years back after ovarian cancer
had had its miserable way with her.
He was a young man then. She was younger.

He clenched his teeth and had her body burned
and paid the bill and hustled back to work
like nothing had happened; like the stone bird

on the still shoulder of her garden saint
which never flew or sang but still remained
solid and silent and ever vigilant

through the slow seasons of his bereavement.
One June for no particular reason
he took the ashes out and scattered them

among her overgrown perennials.
And once the trees were pruned and weeds were pulled,
the birdbath and all the bird feeders filled,

Frank sat alone and wept inconsolably
and prayed to be an instrument of peace
and wondered if only a saint or a sissy

or someone crazy with the loss of love
would labor so to keep something alive?
One day he swore he saw the statue move.

Bird Fishing

The snowy egret at the water's edge
wades with murder in its eyes
among the reeds and mucky riverbed
its great neck curling like a cast
uncurling through a hatch of flies.
And when the muddy water flashes
it stabs its sharp face in a spasm
of hunger splashing fishwards, comes up fed;
and making for stillwater downstream spreads
its white benediction, rises, rises.

Aubade

When he was finished hitting her he went
to work. She woke the boys, sent them to school,
then hung herself with a belt she'd bought him
for his birthday. He would never get it.

Local Obits

It was the Alzheimer's made Maurice sweet
those last ten years in contrast with the six
decades and then some of huffing and puffing
his way through three marriages, a couple of
unsuccessful runs for public office,
his business and the love of his children.
"God's Will" is what his only daughter called it,
to see that awful, angry man gone soft,
gone simple and benevolent at last.
"You take the good with the bad," she reckoned.
"He didn't know me at the end, but he approved."

Couplets

Two girls found dead. My sons go to the morgue.
Two cots, thick rubber gloves, two body bags.

Too long stuffed in a culvert, raped and stabbed,
too decomposed to recognize. Too sad.

Two local ne'er-do-wells no doubt abused
too much as children themselves, stand mute.

Two caskets in a room, two families undone.
Two ministers. Two homilies. My sons

too busy with flowers and townspeople
to contemplate the problem of evil,

to shake their fists at God, regard instead
two funerals—the living and the dead

to be transported in their separate griefs—
two hearses to be washed, two limousines.

Today the wakes and paperwork details.
Tomorrow a burning and a burial.

Two girls found dead of known brutalities
together forever, precious memories

————

too sweet, too savage, too beautiful and bad
to keep at bay by ritual or words.

Two boys about their father's business learn
to number, comfort, witness and keep track.

Still Life in Milford—Oil on Canvas by Lester Johnson

You're lucky to live in a town like this
with art museums and Indian food
and movie houses showing foreign films
and grad students and comely undergrads.
Years back I'd often make the half-hour trip.
It was good for my creative juices
to browse the holy books at Shaman Drum.
Still, life in Milford isn't all that bad.

We have two trendy restaurants and a bar
well known by locals for its Coney dogs.
We have a bookshop now. We even have
a rush hour, art fairs and bon vivants.
And a classic car show every October—
mostly muscle cars—Dodges, Chevys, Fords.
No psychic healers yet or homeopaths.
Still, life in Milford has a certain ambiance,

more Wyeth than Picasso, to be sure,
more meatloaf and potatoes than dim-sum. Fact is,
at first I thought this Lester Johnson was
a shirttail cousin of the Johnson brothers—
long-standing members of the Chamber of Commerce
in Milford, Michigan, like me. In fact
his only connection to these parts was
Still Life in Milford, gathering dust here

---

in the basement of the art museum.
His own Milford's somewhere back east, near Yale—
the day job, teaching, he could never quit
the way that Robert Frost taught English here
and Donald Hall before the muse in them
escaped their offices in Angell Hall.
They were last seen running and maybe running still.
Life in Milford, Michigan, is similar.

I have steady work, a circle of friends
and lunch on Thursdays with the Rotary.
I have a wife, unspeakably beautiful,
a daughter and three sons, a cat, a car,
good credit, taxes and mortgage payments
and certain duties here. Notably,
when folks get horizontal, breathless, still:
life in Milford ends. They call. I send a car.

Between the obsequies I play with words.
I count the sounds and syllables and rhymes.
I try to give it shape and sense, like so:
eight stanzas of eight lines apiece, let's say
ten syllables per line or twelve. Just words.
And if rhyming's out of fashion, I fashion rhymes
that keep their distance, four lines apart, like so.
Still, life in Milford keeps repeating. Say

———

I'm just like Lester, just like Frost and Hall:
I covet the moment in which nothing moves
and crave the life free of life's distractions.
A bucket of flowers on a table.
A vase to arrange the flowers in. A small
pipe—is it?—smoldering in an ashtray to
suggest the artist and impending action.
Still Life in Milford seems a parable

on the human hunger for creation.
The flowers move from bucket to vase
like moving words at random into song—
the act of ordering is all the same—
the ordinary becomes a celebration.
Whether paper, canvas, ink or oil paints,
once finished we achieve a peace we call
Still Life in Milford. Then we sign our names.

Notes

Certain of these poems take, for their titles, the names of Gregorian hymns in Latin. These plain chants were common to the Roman Catholic liturgies until the early 1960s when the Second Vatican Council Englished everything. When I was a child, Latin was the language of faith and adoration. It was mysterious, magical, sacred and dead. I recommend *Chants of the Church* edited and compiled by the Monks of Solemes, published in 1953 by the Gregorian Institute, from which the following interlinear translations are taken:

Attende Domine et miserere: Attend O Lord, and have mercy
Pange lingua: Sing (my) tongue
Inviolata, integra, et casta: Inviolate, untouched, chaste
Panis Angelicus: Bread of Angels
O Gloriosa Virginum: O (thou) glorious among virgins
Parce Domine mei: Spare me Lord
Veni, Creator Spiritus: Come Creator Spirit
Adoro te devote, latens Deitas: I adore thee devoutly hidden Deity
In Paradisum, deducant te: Into paradise be thou conducted

Moveen is a townland on the westernmost peninsula of County Clare. I keep a cottage there that my great-great-grandparents were given when they married. Their son, Tomas, left there late in the nineteenth century and came to Michigan. His niece, Nora Lynch, lived all but a few years of the twentieth century there, tending to her parents in their age, keeping cows, saving hay, outliving her siblings in Ireland and America. She never married. After Tommy, the last of her brothers, died in 1971, she lived alone. She died in 1992. She is buried in the graveyard at Moyarta near the estuarial village of Carrigaholt. She left her home to me. *P 5 2*

"One of Jack's" owes its text to autopsy notes in the files of the Oakland County Medical Examiner's Office to which the bodies of Jack Kevorkian's victims or patients are taken for post mortem examinations. *P 96*

Lester Johnson was born in Minnesota in 1919 and lived, for years, in Milford, Connecticut, while he taught at Yale and where he painted *Still Life in Milford* in 1965. It became part of the permanent collection at the University of Michigan Museum of Art in 1987, the gift of President and Mrs. Harold Shapiro. His work has also been collected by the Museum of Modern Art, Yale, the Walker Art Center and The Detroit Institute of Arts. One door north of the University of Michigan Museum of Art on State Street in Ann Arbor is Angell Hall, which houses the offices of the English Department where Robert Frost and Donald Hall (to name but two among the many greats) put in their time on the faculty there. And one block north of Angell Hall is a bookstore, Shaman Drum, and thirty miles north of Shaman Drum and a little east is Milford, Michigan, where there is, I am obliged to report, still life. *134*

—TL

About the Author

Thomas Lynch is the author of *Skating with Heather Grace* and *Grimalkin & Other Poems*. A collection of his essays, *The Undertaking—Life Studies from the Dismal Trade*, published in 1997, was a finalist for the National Book Award and was awarded an American Book Award and The Heartland Prize for nonfiction. His work has appeared in *The London Review of Books*, *Harper's*, *The New Yorker*, *The Paris Review*, *Poetry*, and elsewhere. He lives and works in Milford, Michigan, where he is the funeral director, and in West Clare where he keeps an ancestral cottage.